THE ADVENT OF
THE PROMISED MESSIAH

The Advent of the Promised Messiah

(Ahmadi Awr Ghayr Ahmadi Mein Kya Farq Hai?)

Hazrat Mirza Ghulam Ahmad

The Promised Messiah and Mahdi
Founder of the Ahmadiyya Muslim Community

ISLAM INTERNATIONAL PUBLICATIONS LIMITED

The Advent of the Promised Messiah

An address by Hazrat Mirza Ghulam Ahmad
The Promised Messiah and Mahdi, peace be upon him,
Founder of the Ahmadiyya Muslim Community

First Published in Urdu in Qadian, India 1906
Present English translation published in the UK 2016

© Islam International Publications Ltd.

Published by:
Islam International Publications Ltd.
Islamabad, Sheephatch Lane
Tilford, Surrey, GU10 2AQ
United Kingdom

Printed and bound by
CPI Group (UK) Ltd, Croydon, CR0 4YY

For more information please visit:
www.alislam.org

ISBN: 978-1-84880-876-8

Contents

Hazrat Mirza Ghulam Ahmad of Qadian
The Promised Messiah & Mahdi
(peace be upon him)

About the Author

Hazrat Mirza Ghulam Ahmad, peace be upon him, was born in 1835 in Qadian, India. From his early life, he dedicated himself to prayer, the study of the Holy Quran and other scriptures. He was deeply pained to observe the plight of Islam, which was being attacked from all directions. In order to defend Islam and present its teachings in their pristine purity, he wrote more than ninety books, thousands of letters and participated in many religious debates. He argued that Islam is a living faith, which can lead humanity to the achievement of moral and spiritual perfection by establishing communion with God.

Hazrat Mirza Ghulam Ahmad, peace be upon him, started experiencing divine dreams, visions and revelations at a young age. In 1889, under divine command, he started accepting initiation into the Ahmadiyya Muslim Community. He continued to receive divine revelations and was thereafter commanded by God to announce that he was the divinely appointed Reformer of the Latter Days, as prophesied by various religions under different titles. He claimed to be the same Promised Messiah and Mahdi whose advent had been prophesied by the Holy Prophet Muhammad, peace and blessings of Allah be upon him. The Ahmadiyya Muslim Community is now established in more than two hundred countries of the world.

After the demise of the Promised Messiah, peace be upon him, in 1908, the institution of *Khilafat* (successorship) was established to continue his mission, in fulfilment of the prophecies made in the Holy Quran and by the Holy Prophet Muhammad, peace and blessings of Allah be upon him. Hazrat Mirza Masroor Ahmad, may Allah be his Helper, is the Fifth Successor to the Promised Messiah, peace be upon him, and the present head of the Ahmadiyya Muslim Community.

Publisher's Note

The words in the text in normal brackets () and in between the long dashes—are the words of the Promised Messiah, peace be upon him, and if any explanatory words or phrases are added by the translator for the purpose of clarification, they are put in square brackets [].

References to the Holy Quran contain the name of the *Surah* [i.e. chapter] followed by a chapter:verse citation, e.g. *Surah Al-Jumu'ah,* 62:4, and counts *Bismillahir-Rahmanir-Rahim* [In the name of Allah the Gracious the Merciful] as the first verse in every chapter it appears.

The name of Muhammad[sa], the Holy Prophet of Islam, has been followed by the symbol [sa], which is an abbreviation for the salutation *Sallallahu Alayhi Wa Sallam* (peace and blessings of Allah be upon him). The names of other Prophets and Messengers are followed by the symbol [as], an abbreviation for *Alayhis-Salam* (peace be upon him). The actual salutations have not generally been set out in full, but they should nevertheless, be understood as being repeated in full in each case.

This is an address by Hazrat Mirza Ghulam Ahmad, peace be upon him, which has been taken and published from *Al-Hakam* (17 February 1906 to 17 June 1906), and at certain places, footnotes are reproduced from *Badr* (26 January 1906 to 23 February 1906).

Previously, this address has also been published in Urdu under the title *Ahmadi Awr Ghayr Ahmadi Mein Kya Farq Hai* i.e. *The Difference between an Ahmadi & a Non-Ahmadi*. However, as per the guidance of Hazrat Khalifatul-Masih V, may Allah be his Helper, it is now being published under the English title *The Advent of the Promised Messiah*.

Publisher

A Note from the Editor of Al-Hakam

This is an address by His Holiness, a Sign of Allah, the Promised Messiah, peace be upon him, delivered in the Aqsa Mosque [1] after *Zuhr* and *Asr* prayers on 27 December 1905.

On the morning of 26 December 1905, a large gathering was held in the main hall of the new guest house, in order to deliberate on the issue relating to the reform of Madrasa Talim-ul-Islam. Many people delivered addresses on various aspects...[2] During the course of this discussion, an individual said:

> *As far as I am aware, the only difference between the community of the Promised Messiah, peace be upon him, and other Muslims is that the latter believe in the Messiah son of Mary having ascended to heaven alive, and we believe that he has passed away. Except*

---

[1] Aqsa Mosque in Qadian, India [Publisher]

[2] Word(s) omitted due to scribal error. [Publisher]

for this, there is no other matter of difference that is contentious in principle between them and us.

As this did not fully represent the purpose of the community's establishment, but rather led to doubt and confusion, it was essential for the Promised Messiah to rectify this notion. As there was insufficient time on the occasion, he thought it appropriate to deliver an address about the real **purpose** of his advent after *Zuhr* and *Asr* prayers on 27th December. Although the Promised Messiah was feeling ill, he gave the following address by the sheer grace and mercy of Allah Almighty. – Editor

The Advent of the Promised Messiah and the Purpose of the Ahmadiyya Muslim Community's Establishment

Unfortunately, at present I am feeling unwell and cannot speak for long. However, due to a matter of importance, I deem it essential to say a few words. Yesterday I heard someone say that the only difference between us and those Muslims who oppose us relates to the life and death of the Messiah, peace be upon him; otherwise, we are one and the same. It is further claimed that as far as the practice of our opponents is concerned, they too are in the right. That is to say, their prayer, fasting and other practices are those of Muslims, and they follow all the injunctions of Islam. The only error that had crept into them related to the demise of Jesus, peace be upon him, and in order to remove this, God Almighty established this community.

However, it ought to be realised that this view is incorrect. Although it is true that this error is rampant among the Muslims, if someone were to presume that **the purpose of my advent in the world** was to rectify this error alone, and there was no other fault among the Muslims that required reformation, rather they are on the right path, then such a notion is false. In my view, the belief relating to the death or life of the Messiah is not of such importance for which Allah the Exalted would have established a community so significant and sent to the world a particular individual to manifest His magnificent glory at a time when darkness had enveloped the world and the earth had become accursed. The error regarding the life of Jesus, peace be upon him, is not one which has arisen in this age, but emerged a short while after the demise of the Holy Prophet, peace and blessings of Allah be upon him; and despite the coming of distinguished holy personages, righteous people and the elect of Allah, people have remained ensnared in this error. If the purpose was to rectify this error alone, Allah the Exalted would have done so at that time, but He did not, and to this day, the aforementioned error has persisted. Even now, if this alone were the only issue, Allah the Exalted would not have established a community for this purpose, as the death of **the Messiah** was not a view that had never been accepted by anyone else in the past. In former times, many of the elect to whom Allah Almighty had disclosed this truth, did believe in the death of Jesus. However, there is another purpose for which Allah the Exalted has established this community. It is true that the removal of the misconception relating to the life of the **Messiah** was also one of the great objectives of establishing this community, but God Almighty has not raised me for this task alone. In fact, many errors had arisen such that if Allah Almighty had not established a community and appointed someone to rectify them, the world would have perished and **Islam** would have been annihilated completely! We can describe this question in another way: what is the purpose of my advent?

The death of Jesus and the life of Islam are two issues which are very closely intertwined. The issue relating to the death of the Messiah has, in this age, become vital for the life of **Islam.** This is because the disorder resulting from the alleged **life of the Messiah** has become immensely widespread.

In order to substantiate that the Messiah is alive, one may perhaps argue as to whether Allah Almighty is powerful enough to have taken him alive to heaven.

However, this demonstrates an ignorance concerning the power of God and His...[1] We, for our part, are foremost in the faith and belief that:

$$ اَنَّ اللّٰهَ عَلٰى كُلِّ شَىْءٍ قَدِيْرٌ $$ [2]

Undoubtedly, Allah the Exalted has power over all things and we believe that He can invariably do whatsoever He wills. However, He is free and pure from such acts that are at variance with His perfect attributes. He is an enemy to all that which opposes His teachings. In earlier times, the doctrine concerning the life of Jesus was just an error, but today, this error has taken on the form of a serpent intent on devouring Islam. In the previous age, there was no fear of any harm on account of this error, as this was nothing more than an inconsequential mistake. But after Christianity **expanded** and its followers began to proclaim that the **life** of the Messiah was a very powerful argument in support of his divinity, this has become a perilous matter. The Christians persistently argue in the most emphatic manner that if the Messiah was not God, how then could he be seated on the **divine throne**? Moreover, if it is within

---

[1] Word(s) omitted due to scribal error. [Publisher]

[2] *al-Baqarah*, 2:107 [Publisher]

the ability of a mortal to ascend to **heaven alive,** why then, until now, has no one ever ascended to heaven since Adam?

With the help of such arguments the Christians wish to deify Jesus, peace be upon him, and so they have done, leading a part of the world astray. A large number of Muslims, reportedly exceeding three million, have fallen victim to this trial through their belief in this false doctrine.

Now if this had been true and if Jesus, peace be upon him, had actually ascended to heaven alive as the Christians assert—and the Muslims support them out of misconception and ignorance—**then this would have been a day of mourning** for Islam. For Islam appeared in the world so that the people may inculcate faith and certainty in the existence of Allah Almighty, and to propagate His Oneness.

No flaw can be found in the religion of Islam, for it is free from all deficiency.[1] It declares Allah the Exalted alone to be One and without partner. To believe that any other being shares this quality is an affront to Allah

---

[1] An authentic copy of the original text of the address [Publisher]

Almighty and Islam does not approve of this. By advocating this 'distinction' of the Messiah, the Christians have misguided the world; and the Muslims, without giving thought to it, readily accept this, being unmindful of the harm this has done to Islam.

One must never be deceived by those who argue as to whether or not Allah the Exalted is powerful enough to have taken the Messiah alive to heaven. There is no doubt that He is **powerful**, but He never permits such things that would become a source of polytheism and which make man a partner with the Creator. And it is clearly evident that attributing certain divine characteristics to a person is clearly a source of associating partners with Allah. Hence, to suggest that the Messiah, peace be upon him, is distinct in that, unlike all others he is still alive and above human limitations, provides the Christians an opportunity to present this argument as proof of his **divinity**.

If by way of allegation, a Christian demanded the Muslims to present any other mortal, who at this time, had ever been endowed with such a distinction, they would have no answer. For these Muslims who oppose us believe that all the Prophets, peace be upon them, have died; yet in their estimation, the death of the Messiah is unfounded. The reason being that they interpret *tawaffa* to mean *ascension to heaven alive.* Therefore, [1] فَلَمَّا تَوَفَّيْتَنِى too, would have to be interpreted in the same sense; that is to say, 'when You raised me to heaven alive.' Furthermore, in their opinion, there is no verse that proves that Jesus would ever die. What then would be the result of this misconception? May Allah the Exalted guide them and may they come to realise their error. I truly say that those who call themselves Muslims, yet do not renounce this doctrine, despite knowing of its flawed and foul nature, are the enemies and **traitors** of Islam.

Bear in mind that Allah Almighty repeatedly speaks of the **death** of the Messiah in the Holy Quran, and establishes that like all other Prophets and humans, he too has passed away. Jesus possessed no distinction that was not shared by other Prophets and human beings. The truth is that *tawaffa* means death. No lexicon confirms that *tawaffa* ever means bodily ascension to heaven. The excellence of a language lies in the universal application of its vocabulary. There is no language in the

---

[1] *al-Ma'idah*, 5:118 [Publisher]

world that makes a distinction between people in the application of a particular term. Of course, such distinction holds with God Almighty, for He is One and without partner. Show me any lexicon which specifically states that *tawaffa* means 'bodily ascension to heaven alive' when used for Jesus but 'death' when it is used for the rest of the world. Show me any lexicon which makes such a distinction, and if you fail to do so—and surely you will—then fear God Almighty because this is a source of associating partners with God. As a result of this very error, the Muslims remain subdued by the Christians.

The Christians could assert that since you consider the Messiah to be alive in heaven, and believe in his return as well, and also that he would come as an Arbitrator, then what doubt remains as regards his divinity, especially when it is not proven that he will ever die? What a pity it would be **if a Christian poses a question and there is no answer.**

Therefore, the evil effect of this error has reached great extremes. It is true that in reality the death of the Messiah was not such a grand issue for which such a grand reformer was required! But I see that the condition of the Muslims has weakened considerably. They no longer ponder over the Holy Quran and their character has fallen to ruins. If their character was appropriate and they had paid due attention to the Holy Quran and its lexicons, they would never have subscribed to such an interpretation. It is for this reason that they, of their own accord, invented the aforementioned meaning. For the word *tawaffa* was not something unique or novel. Every Arabic lexicon, by every author, defines it as **'death'**. Why then have they invented, of their own fancy, the meaning of *bodily ascension to heaven*? I would have no regret if they had applied this word in a similar sense to the Holy Prophet, peace and blessings of Allah be upon him, as well. This is because the very same word has also been used for him in the Holy Quran, as it is stated:

وَ اِمَّا نُرِيَنَّكَ بَعْضَ الَّذِىْ نَعِدُهُمْ اَوْ نَتَوَفَّيَنَّكَ [1]

Now if this word truly means *bodily ascension to heaven,* are we not justified in applying the same sense to the

---

[1] And if We show thee *in thy lifetime the fulfilment of* some of the things with which We have threatened them, *thou wilt know it;* or if We cause thee to die before that... (*Yunus,* 10:47) [Publisher]

9

Holy Prophet as well? Why is it that when this term is used for a Prophet, who is thousands of times lower in rank than the Holy Prophet, peace and blessings of Allah be upon him, the self-concocted definition of, 'ascension to heaven alive,' is applied, but when the word refers to the Chief of All Ages, we take it to mean nothing but death? In fact, it is the Holy Prophet[sa] who is a Living Prophet and his **life** is established to such a degree as is not the case with any other Prophet. Therefore, we strongly and emphatically claim that **if there is a Prophet who lives, it is our Noble Prophet, peace and blessings of Allah be upon him,** and none other. Many prominent scholars have written books on **the Prophet** being alive and I possess such outstanding proofs of his life that no one can contest in this regard.

With all this, another point is that a living prophet can only be one whose **blessings** and **bounties** are forever flowing. We find that since the time of the Holy Prophet to the present age, Allah Almighty has never forsaken the Muslims, and at the turn of each **century,** He sent a person who reformed the people in keeping with the demands of the time. And now, in this century He **has sent me** so that I may establish that **the Prophet lives.**

It is also confirmed by the Holy Quran that Allah the Exalted has always and shall continue to safeguard the religion of the Holy Prophet, peace and blessings of Allah be upon him, as He states:

إِنَّا نَحْنُ نَزَّلْنَا الذِّكْرَ وَ إِنَّا لَهُ لَحَفِظُونَ ¹

Meaning, *'Verily, We, Ourselves, have sent down this Exhortation and most surely We shall safeguard it.'*

The words ² إِنَّا لَهُ لَحَفِظُونَ clearly show that such persons shall continue to come at the turn of the century who would bring back the lost glory of Islam and guide the people.

It is a matter of principle that with the passage of each century, the existing generation also leaves this world. The scholars, the *Huffaz*³ of the Quran, and the holy and pious people of that generation all pass away. Hence, the need arises for a person to be raised in order to revive the religion of Islam; otherwise this **religion** would perish if a new arrangement was not made to keep

---

¹ *al-Hijr*, 15:10 [Publisher]
² Most surely We shall safeguard it. (*al-Hijr*, 15:10) [Publisher]
³ People who have committed the Holy Quran to memory. [Publisher]

it pure in subsequent centuries. For this reason, at the turn of every century, God appoints a person who saves Islam from dying, and grants it new life, and safeguards the world from the errors, religious innovations, negligence and indolence that have crept into the people.

The Holy Prophet, peace and blessings of Allah be upon him, alone enjoys this distinction, and this is such a convincing proof of his **life** that no one can contest in this regard. In light of this, the stream of his **blessings and bounties** are limitless and unending. Moreover, in every age, it is through him that the **Ummah** is **blessed,** and it is through him that they are taught, thus becoming the beloved of Allah Almighty, as He states:

اِنْ كُنْتُمْ تُحِبُّوْنَ اللهَ فَاتَّبِعُوْنِيْ يُحْبِبْكُمُ اللهُ [1]

So, it is evident that the love of God Almighty has never abandoned this Ummah in any century, and this very fact alone serves as a brilliant argument in favour of the **life** of the Holy Prophet, peace and blessings of Allah be upon him. On the contrary, the life of Jesus is not established. Even during his lifetime such disorder

---

[1] If you love Allah, follow me: *then* will Allah love you. (*Al-e-Imran*, 3:32) [Publisher]

erupted as was unprecedented in the life of any other Prophet. This is why Allah Almighty felt the need to inquire from Jesus[as],

ءَاَنْتَ قُلْتَ لِلنَّاسِ اتَّخِذُوْنِیْ وَ اُمِّیَ الٰهَیْنِ [1]

That is to say, was it you who told the people, 'Take me and my mother for God'? The community that Jesus[as] established was so weak and unreliable that even the Christians themselves admit this fact. The Gospel corroborates that of the twelve disciples, who were the embodiment of the distinct spiritual power and influence of Jesus, one was **Judas Iscariot**, who sold his master and guide for thirty pieces of silver. Another who was greatest in rank and was known as his foremost disciple, and in whose hands were the keys of Paradise, namely Peter, **cursed** Jesus three times while standing before him. If this was the influence and grace of the Messiah in his own lifetime, one can only imagine what remains after 1900 years?

In comparison, the community built by the Holy Prophet, peace and blessings of Allah be upon him, was so **faithful** and **loyal** that they sacrificed their lives,

---

[1] *al-Ma'idah,* 5:117 [Publisher]

13

abandoned their homelands and left their kith and kin for his sake. In short, they gave no importance to anything over him. How remarkable was this influence! Even adversaries admit this fact. And indeed, his ongoing influence has not halted, rather flows forth even today.

The teaching of the Holy Quran still possesses the same influence and the same blessings as before. Another example of this, which is worthy of mention, is that nothing is known about the whereabouts of the Gospel. Even the Christians themselves are faced with difficulties in determining the origins of the Gospel, its original language, and where it is now. However, the Holy Quran has always been protected. Not even a single word or dot can be altered. It has been guarded to the extent that *Huffaz* of the Holy Quran, numbering in the hundreds of thousands, are present in every country and nation, and there is complete consensus between them. They continue to memorise the Holy Quran and recite it to others. Now reflect, are these blessings of the Holy Prophet not ever-living? Do they not prove that the Holy Prophet **lives**?

Hence, whether in view of the protection of the Holy Quran; or whether in light of the Hadith on the coming of reformers at the turn of each century for the revival of religion; or whether on account of his blessings and influence, which continue even to this day; it is established that the Holy Prophet **lives.**

Now, the point to ponder is what benefit the doctrine relating to the **life** of Jesus has brought to the world? Has it resulted in moral and practical reform or has it given rise to evil? The more one ponders over this fact, the defects of this doctrine become all the more evident. I truly say that Islam has sustained immense harm owing to this doctrine, so much so that nearly four hundred million people have converted to Christianity. They have forsaken the true God to deify a humble mortal. The 'benefit' which Christianity has brought to the world is apparent. The Christians themselves have admitted that many immoralities have spread in the world due to Christianity. For when one is taught that their sins are now the burden of another, such a person becomes audacious in committing sin. Indeed, sin is a lethal poison for mankind, which has been spread by Christianity. Such being the case, the harm of this doctrine continues to increase manifold.

I do not say that the people of this age are at fault alone for believing in **the life of the Messiah**. Nay, some among the people of past too were mistaken, but even in their error they remained worthy of divine reward. For it is written قَدْ يُخْطِئُ وَيُصِيْبُ, that is, on certain occasions a *Mujtahid*[1] errs and on other occasions he is in the right. But in both cases he receives divine reward. The fact is that this matter remained hidden from them because this is what divine will had so desired. Thus, they remained in ignorance and, like the People of the Cave,[2] this truth was not disclosed to them. In this context, I also received the revelation:

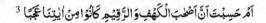

اَمْ حَسِبْتَ اَنَّ اَصْحٰبَ الْكَهْفِ وَالرَّقِيْمِ كَانُوْا مِنْ اٰيٰتِنَا عَجَبًا [3]

---

[1] A scholar of Islam who strives to come to a conclusion on religious matters on the basis of his own analytical reasoning, in light of the fundamental sources of Islam, namely, the Holy Quran, Sunnah and Hadith. [Publisher]

[2] The People of the Cave is a reference to the early Christians who took refuge in catacombs to save themselves from persecution at the hands of various idolatrous emperors. For more information please see *Short English Commentary of the Holy Quran* by Malik Ghulam Farid under chapter 18 verse 10. [Publisher]

[3] Do you think that the People of the Cave and the Inscription were a wonder among Our Signs? [Publisher]

Similarly, the issue relating to the life of the Messiah is a remarkable secret. The Holy Quran clearly and lucidly establishes the death of the Messiah and the Hadith also substantiate this fact. Further, the verse that was recited to deduce the same, on the day that the Holy Prophet, peace and blessings of Allah be upon him, passed away also confirms this.[1] However, despite this matter being so manifest, God Almighty **concealed** it, and kept it hidden for the Promised One. And so when he appeared, **he disclosed this secret**.

In His wisdom, whenever Allah Almighty so wills, He conceals a secret or unveils it. Thus, He kept this matter hidden until its appointed **time**, but now when the Promised One has appeared, in his hand was <u>the key to this **secret**, and so he revealed it. Now, anyone who does not accept this and remains obstinate, wars with Allah Almighty</u>.

Therefore, the issue of the Messiah's death has become a matter that is no longer shrouded in any obscurity; rather, it has become clear in every respect. The Holy Quran establishes the death of the Messiah and the

---

[1] And Muhammad is only a Messenger. Verily, *all* Messengers have passed away before him. (*Al-e-Imran*, 3:145) [Publisher]

Hadith also lend support to this. Moreover, the incident of the *Mi'raj*[1] of the Holy Prophet, peace and blessings of Allah be upon him, also testifies to the Messiah's death. The Holy Prophet[sa] gives eye-witness testimony as it were, because he saw Jesus[as] and John[as] together on the night of the *Mi'raj*. Likewise, there is the following verse:

$$\text{قُلْ سُبْحَانَ رَبِّیْ هَلْ كُنْتُ اِلَّا بَشَرًا رَسُوْلًا}^{2}$$

This also bars the Messiah from ascending to heaven alive. For, when the disbelievers demanded the Holy Prophet to show a miracle by ascending to heaven, Allah the Exalted gave him the answer:

$$\text{قُلْ سُبْحَانَ رَبِّیْ هَلْ كُنْتُ اِلَّا بَشَرًا رَسُوْلًا}^{3}$$

That is to say, my Lord is above and beyond going back on His promise. For He has already decreed that human beings are born in this very world and it is here that they shall die. God states:

---

[1] A spiritual experience of the Holy Prophet[sa] where he ascended to the heavens. [Publisher]

[2] Say, 'Holy is my Lord! I am not but a man *sent as a* Messenger. (*Bani Isra'il*, 17:94) [Publisher]

[3] Ibid.

$$\text{فِيهَا تَحْيَوْنَ وَفِيهَا تَمُوتُونَ}^{1}$$

I am not but a man sent as a messenger, i.e. I possess limitations of human nature, which keep me from ascending to heaven. In fact, the disbelievers had posed this question deliberately, for they had already heard that a human lives and dies on this earth. Therefore, they took their opportunity and posed this question. However, the answer given to them frustrated their design. Therefore, it is already a settled matter that the Messiah[as] has passed away. It is indeed a miraculous sign that the people were kept in ignorance to this fact and the wise were kept oblivious.

Do bear in mind that those who passed on before the present **age** are excused, for this matter was not proved to them categorically. They shall receive their reward and recompense from Allah Almighty for what they interpreted in their time according to their own earnest judgement. **However,** now that age is over. In this age, Allah Almighty has lifted the veil and has revealed this hidden secret together with the evil and dangerous implications of the issue at hand. You see that Islam is in

---

[1] Therein shall you live, and therein shall you die. (*al-A'raf,* 7:26) [Publisher]

a state of decline and the Christians continue to attack Islam with this very **weapon of the life of the Messiah.** Muslim progeny is falling prey to the Christians. I truthfully say that it is arguments such as these, which they put forth to the people so as to convert them. They are turning people away from Islam by quoting in schools and colleges the distinct qualities which the Muslims ascribe to Jesus in their ignorance. Therefore, <u>God Almighty has desired that now the Muslims be warned</u>.[1]

Since, God has desired to make the Muslims vigilant, it is very important for the **progress of Islam** to emphasise the issue relating to the death of the Messiah and for the Muslims not to believe that **the Messiah has ascended to heaven alive**. Regrettably, I must say that my opponents, owing to their own misfortune, fail to understand this secret and raise a pointless clamour. If only these fools would realise that if we all laid stress on the death of Jesus[as], the Christian faith would be no more. I proclaim with certainty that the life of Islam lies in this **death**. Ask the Christians themselves: if it is proved that the Messiah lives no more and has died,

---

[1] *Al-Hakam*, Volume 10, No. 6, dated 17 February 1906, pp. 2-3

what would remain of their religion? They themselves are convinced that it is this very issue which uproots their religion. Yet the Muslims give them strength by believing in the life of the Messiah, and thus cause harm to Islam. Their example may be described as such:

یکے بر سر شاخ و بن سے برید [1]

These Muslims have taken hold of [2] the very same weapon that the Christians use against Islam, and wielded it foolishly without understanding, thus inflicting severe injury on Islam. However, it is a matter of jubilation that Allah the Exalted has informed them of this at **precisely the correct** time and has armed them with a matchless weapon to break the cross; in order to reinforce it and make use of it, He has established this Community. As such, by the grace and succour of Allah Almighty, this weapon, namely the **death of the Messiah,** has left the religion of the cross so weak and

---

[1] A person who saws off the same branch on which he sits. [Publisher]

[2] **Footnote:** *Badr* states, 'It is astonishing that the Christians use this weapon in order to cut the necks of the Muslims, and the Muslims too come forth to support them in doing so.' (*Badr*, Volume 2, No. 4, dated 26 January 1906, p. 3)

powerless that now this is not hidden to anyone. The Christians and their supporters are well aware that if there is any sect or community that can uproot their religion it is **this Community**. This is why the Christians are eager to compete with the people of every other religion, but dare not face this Community. When a certain Bishop was invited to compete, he did not come forward to contest, even though various English newspapers urged him to accept the challenge. The reason for this is that we possess such weapons to uproot Christianity, which have not been given to others, the first of which is the weapon of the Messiah's death. To prove him dead is not the real objective. This was merely a weapon of the Christians that inflicted harm upon Islam. Allah the Exalted desired to rectify this error, and so was it done in the most emphatic of ways.

Aside from this, another of our chief objectives is to remove the errors and self-invented beliefs that have crept into Islam. It would be unwise to suggest that there was no difference whatsoever between this Community and other Muslims. If the Muslims of today have remained unchanged in their beliefs and both are one and the same, then did God the Exalted establish this Community in vain? To entertain such a notion is a great dishonour to this Community, as well as an act of temerity and insolence in the face of Allah the Exalted. For He has repeatedly expressed that darkness has engulfed the world both in respect of practice and doctrine.

Countless Prophets and Messengers appeared in the world, and tirelessly toiled and strove to establish the Oneness of Allah, but today a dark veil has been drawn over it. Further, the people have fallen victim to various forms of polytheism. The Holy Prophet, peace and blessings of Allah be upon him, enjoined that one ought not to love the world, but today, the love of the world dominates every heart and everyone seems immersed in this very love. When asked, some are averse to under-taking even an iota of work for the sake of religion, reluctance holds them back and they begin to invent thousands of excuses. Every form of misconduct and immorality is considered permissible and every possible transgression is brazenly committed. Religion has become fatally weak and stands helpless like an orphan. In this state, if Islam had not been helped and supported, when else was it to confront such circumstances as would lend reason for its support? Islam remains only in name. If even now it were not afforded protection, it would undoubtedly perish.

I truthfully say that only a lack of understanding prompts the question as to whether there is any difference between our community and other Muslims. If only one such matter existed, what need was there for such effort and why establish an entire community? I am aware that Allah Almighty has repeatedly disclosed that darkness has fallen and nothing can be seen. The Oneness of God which was once our crown and the pride of Islam has now been reduced to mere lip service. Otherwise, there are perhaps very few who really profess the Oneness of God in terms of practice and belief. The Holy Prophet[sa] advised that one ought not to love the world, but now every heart is engrossed therein. Religion has become helpless as though it were an orphan. The Holy Prophet, peace and blessings of Allah be upon him, clearly said:

$$\text{حُبُّ الدُّنْيَا رَأْسُ كُلِّ خَطِيئَةٍ}^{1}$$

How pure and true is this phrase. But observe now and you will find everyone is victim to this error. Our Arya

---

[1] Love of the world is the root cause of all vice. [Publisher]

and Christian opponents have very well come to know the reality of their religions, and yet they cling to them. The Christians are well aware that the principles and doctrines of their religion are improper and that it is inappropriate to deify a human being. In this age, knowledge of philosophy, physics and science has advanced greatly and people have come to realise clearly that the Messiah was but a weak and frail mortal who did not possess any supernatural power whatsoever. After having studied these sciences, in light of one's personal experiences, and in view of the weaknesses and frailties of the Messiah, it is impossible to believe that he was God. Never in the least.

Associating partners with God began and was founded at the hand of a woman; that is, **Eve**, who followed the command of Satan instead of God Almighty. And now too it is women who support this great form of polytheism—Christianity. In all truth, the Christian religion is one which human nature repels from afar and can never accept. Were it not for worldly motives, a large majority of Christians today would have become Muslim. In fact, some among the Christians have been Muslims in secret. They concealed their belief, but at the time of death proclaimed that they were Muslims when leaving behind their wills. There were very high ranking officials among these people as well. They did not reveal that they were Muslims during their life out of their love for the world, but ultimately, they conceded this fact. I see that Islam has found way into their hearts and now it continues to flourish. The love of this world has blinded the people.

In short, it is this very love of the world that has caused internal dissent among the Muslims as well. For if the pleasure of Allah Almighty had taken precedence it could easily be ascertained as to which sect possessed sounder principles, and by accepting them, everyone could have reunited. Now, in view of this shortcoming, caused by the love of this world, how can these people be called Muslims? For they do not follow in the footsteps of the Holy Prophet, peace and blessings of Allah be upon him. As such, Allah Almighty has said:

قُلْ اِنْ كُنْتُمْ تُحِبُّوْنَ اللهَ فَاتَّبِعُوْنِىْ يُحْبِبْكُمُ اللهُ [1]

Meaning, Say, 'If you love Allah Almighty then obey me, and God will in turn befriend you.' But now it is **the love of this world** that is given precedence over **love for**

---

[1] *Al-e-Imran,* 3:32 [Publisher]

Allah and following the Messenger of Allah, peace and blessings of Allah be upon him. Is this obedience to the Holy Prophet, peace and blessings of Allah be upon him? Was the Holy Prophet, peace and blessings of Allah be upon him, a worldly man? Would he accept interest? Was he negligent in carrying out his obligations and in fulfilling divine commandments? Was he (God-forbid) a hypocrite? Would he compromise on matters of principle? Did he give precedence to the world over religion? One ought to reflect.

Obedience means to follow in the footsteps of the Holy Prophet[sa]. Then behold how Allah Almighty showers His blessings. The Companions of the Holy Prophet[sa] acted in this manner and witness how Allah Almighty rewarded them with immense success! They turned their backs to the world and completely renounced its allure. They extinguished their desires. Now compare your state with theirs. Do you follow in their footsteps? Alas! Today, people do not realise what God Almighty desires of them. Indeed [1] رَأْسُ كُلِّ خَطِيئَةٍ [love of the world] has spawned many a child. People go to court and do not feel the least bit of shame or regret in bearing false

---

[1] The root cause of all vice. [Publisher]

testimony for a mere two *annas*. Can advocates declare on oath that all the witnesses they produce in court are truthful? Today, the state of the world has become dire in every respect. False witnesses are produced, lodging false lawsuits is nothing, and false certificates are forged. Whenever people speak, they steer clear of the truth. Now, one must ask these people, who see no need in establishing this community, is this the **religion** which the Holy Prophet, peace and blessings of Allah be upon him, brought? Allah the Exalted equates falsehood to filth and states that one ought to abstain from it:

اِجْتَنِبُوا الرِّجْسَ مِنَ الْأَوْثَانِ وَ اجْتَنِبُوْا قَوْلَ الزُّوْرِ ¹

Here falsehood is mentioned with idolatry. Just as a foolish person abandons Allah Almighty and bows before stone, so does one shun truth and piety to achieve his own ends, and take **falsehood** as an idol. This is the very reason that Allah the Exalted has mentioned falsehood alongside idol-worship and drawn a parallel between the two. Just as an idol-worshipper seeks salvation from an idol, a liar also carves an idol and surmises that they shall be delivered through this idol. How

---

¹ Shun therefore the abomination of idols, and shun false speech. (*al-Hajj*, 22:31) [Publisher]

rampant has evil become? It is a pity that when people are asked the reason for their being idolaters and are advised to shun this abomination, they say that they cannot, and that they have no other option. What can be more unfortunate than the fact that such people consider their lives to be wholly reliant on falsehood? I assure you, however, that ultimately truth prevails, and goodness and success belong to it alone.

I remember that once I sent an article to Amritsar along with a letter, which was related to the Wakil-i-Hind newspaper owned by Ralia Ram. This letter was deemed to be in contravention of the postal laws and so a lawsuit was filed against me. Even my lawyers advised that there was no hope of acquittal unless the letter was denied, that is to say, there was no way of escape except through untruth. However, I did not approve of this in the least and said that if I am punished for speaking the truth then so be it, I shall not lie. The lawsuit was finally heard in court and the superintendent of post offices appeared as the plaintiff. When I was questioned about this, I honestly replied that the letter was mine but that I had placed it along with the article, considering it to be a part thereof. Allah Almighty granted insight to the magis-

trate and so he understood this point. The superintendent of post offices exerted his best efforts but the
magistrate paid no heed and acquitted me.[1]

---

[1] *Badr* records this incident in detail as follows:

Approximately 27 or 28 years ago or perhaps even earlier, I
dispatched an article in support of Islam against the Aryas for
printing in a press owned by a Christian named Ralia Ram, a lawyer
residing in Amritsar. He was also the proprietor of a newspaper. The
article was sent in a postal packet open on both sides and I also placed
a letter in the packet. This letter contained statements in support of
Islam and the falsity of other faiths, as well as an emphatic request for
the article to be printed. For this reason the Christian [editor]
became inflamed on account of his religious opposition. It so
happened that on this occasion, he found an opportunity to make a
hostile attack against me, as the postal law stipulated that it was an
offence punishable by a fine of up to 500 rupees or with up to six-
month imprisonment, to place such a letter in a postal packet.
However, I was utterly unaware of this. He acted as an informant to
the postal authorities and had a case filed against me.

Before I received intimation of this case, Allah the Exalted revealed
to me in a dream that the lawyer Ralia Ram had sent a serpent my
way to bite me but I fried the serpent like fish and sent it back to him.
I am certain that this was an indication that the decision given in
court on this case might become a precedent for lawyers. In short, I
was summoned to Gurdaspur (the headquarters of the district) to
defend this charge. All the lawyers that were consulted regarding this
case, advised that the only way of escape was to lie, and suggested for
me to plead that I had not put the letter in the packet, and that Ralia
Ram himself must have placed it therein. The lawyers assured me
that in such case a verdict would be issued on the basis of testimony.

How can I say that one cannot do without lying? Such notions are sheer absurdity. The reality is that one

---

Moreover, they said that acquittal could be secured with two or three false witnesses, otherwise the case was a difficult one, with no hope of escape. I told them all categorically that I would not swerve an inch from the truth, come what may. On the very same day or maybe a day after, I appeared in the court of an English magistrate and a superintendent of the post offices appeared as the plaintiff on behalf of the government. The magistrate proceeded to record my statement. The very first question he asked me was, *'Did you put this letter in the packet and were the letter and packet dispatched by you?'* I answered without any hesitation whatsoever, *'This is my letter and this is my packet. I myself placed the letter in the packet when I sent it, but I did not do this with any ill-intent to cause loss of revenue to the government. I did not consider the letter distinct and separate from the article enclosed in the packet, nor did the letter contain any personal matter.'* On hearing this, God Almighty inclined the heart of the magistrate towards me. The superintendent of post offices created an uproar against me, and made long speeches in English, which I could not follow, except that each time he made a point, the magistrate would reject it saying, *'No, no.'* When the superintendent concluded his submission and finished venting his anger, the magistrate turned to write his verdict. After writing a line or two, he said, *'Alright, you may leave.'* Hearing this, I came out of the court room thanking my truly benevolent God, Who had upheld me in opposition to an English officer. I know full well that on this occasion, God Almighty delivered me from this misfortune due to the blessings of truthfulness. Before this case, I had seen in a dream that a man stretched forth his hand to take off my cap, whereupon I said, *'What are you doing?'* At this, he left the cap on my head and

cannot do without truth. Even today when I recall this incident, it gives me pleasure. I followed the command of God Almighty and He favoured me in such a manner as to become a sign.

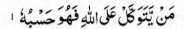

Remember well that nothing is more unblessed than falsehood. Generally, worldly people say that those who speak the truth are arrested, but how can I agree? Seven lawsuits have been filed against me and by the grace of God Almighty I have not had to give a single false statement in any one of them. Can anyone point out a single case in which God Almighty caused me to suffer defeat? Allah Almighty Himself defends and supports the truth. Is it possible that He should punish a righteous person? Were it so, no one on earth would dare speak the truth, belief in God Almighty would die out and the virtuous would die a living death.

---

said, *'It is fine, it is fine.'* (*Badr*, Volume 2, No. 5, dated 2 February 1906, p. 3)

[1] And he who puts his trust in Allah – He is sufficient for him. (*at-Talaq*, 65:4) [Publisher]

The fact is that those who are punished for speaking the truth are not penalised because they have adhered to honesty; rather, they are punished on account of certain other hidden vices or for having lied at some other occasion. God Almighty knows of countless other sins and vices committed by such people. Their wrongdoings are many and it is on account of one or the other that they are punished.

One of my teachers, Gul Ali Shah resided in Batala and also used to teach Partab Singh, the son of Sher Singh. He states that on one occasion Sher Singh beat his cook severely only on account of using an excess of salt and pepper. Since Gul Ali Shah was a simple person, he protested to Sher Singh that he had ill-treated the cook. Sher Singh replied, *'Maulvi Ji is unaware that this man has stolen one hundred goats from me.'* Similarly, man indulges in a plethora of evil deeds, but he is caught on a particular occasion and then punished.[1]

A person who speaks the truth can never be disgraced for he basks in the protection of God Almighty. There is no fortress or citadel more secure than the protection

---

[1] *Badr* states, 'Man sins on a certain occasion and is caught on another.' (*Badr*, Volume 2, No. 6, dated 9 February 1906, p. 3)

of God Almighty. Half-hearted effort, however, brings no benefit. Would anyone suggest that when a person is thirsty, to drink one drop would suffice; or in the case of extreme hunger, one gram or morsel would satisfy? On the contrary, until such a person drinks or eats their fill, they will not be satisfied. Similarly, until actions are performed to perfection they do not yield the fruits or benefits that are expected. Flawed actions neither please Allah Almighty nor can they be blessed. Allah Almighty promises to grant blessings only when deeds are performed according to His will.

Therefore, worldly people themselves invent such notions that one cannot live without resorting to falsehood and deception. Some say that such and such person was sentenced to four years for speaking the truth in a lawsuit, but I reiterate that these are all baseless notions arising out of a lack of insight.

کسب کمال کن کہ عزیزے جہاں شوی[1]

All this is the result of weakness. Perfection does not yield such fruits. Just because a person can mend his own

---

[1] Attain excellence so that you become endeared to the world. [Publisher]

coarse cotton cloak, this does not make them a tailor, and does not guarantee that they will also be able to sew high quality silk clothes. If such clothes are given to such a person, ultimately he will ruin them. Thus, virtue adulterated with filth is useless and amounts to nothing before God Almighty. But these people take pride in this and seek salvation through it. If there is sincerity, Allah the Exalted does not allow even an iota of goodness to be lost. He Himself says:

$$ مَنْ يَّعْمَلْ مِثْقَالَ ذَرَّةٍ خَيْرًا يَّرَهُ \,^1 $$

Therefore, even a grain of goodness will be rewarded by Allah Almighty. Why then is it that even after performing virtue some are not rewarded? This is because their actions lack sincerity. Indeed, sincerity is the prerequisite for deeds. It is stated:

$$ مُخْلِصِيْنَ لَهُ الدِّيْنَ \,^2 $$

Such sincerity is to be found in the elect of God.[3] Those who act in this manner become the chosen ones of God and no longer remain of this world. Their every action

---

[1] Then whoso does an atom's weight of good will see it. (*az-Zilzal*, 99:8) [Publisher]

[2] Being sincere to Him in obedience. (*al-Bayyinah*, 98:6) [Publisher]

[3] *Al-Hakam,* Volume 10, No. 17, dated 17 May 1906, pp. 4-5

possesses sincerity and worth. However, the case of worldly people is that even when they give alms they do so only to seek praise and admiration. If they give charity for a meritorious cause, their only object is to be praised by the newspapers and the public. What relation does such 'virtue' have with God Almighty? Many people marry and give a feast to the whole village, but not for the sake of God, only as an expression of vanity and to seek acclaim. Had there not been such ostentation and had this action been performed out of sheer compassion for Allah's creation, and purely for His sake, these people would have become saints. However, as such actions have no relation or connection with God Almighty, therefore, they fail to produce any good and blessed effect.

Know well that God Almighty becomes one with those who become His. God cannot be deceived by anyone. It is utterly foolish and absurd for one to surmise that they can fool God through pretence and deception. Such people only deceive themselves. The allure and love of the world is the root of all vice. Blinded by it, a person loses their humanity and does not realise what they are doing and what they ought to have done. When even a wise person cannot be deceived by another, how can

Allah Almighty fall prey to deception? Indeed, it is the love of this world which lies at the root of such evil deeds. In this vein, the cardinal sin, which in this age has led the Muslims to their ruinous state and to which they are a victim, is none other than this same love of the world.

Whether sleeping or awake, standing, sitting or walking, in every state, people are gripped by this very worry and distress. They have no concern or regard for the time when they shall be lowered into their graves. If such people feared Allah Almighty and possessed even little concern and grief for religion, they could have benefitted immensely. Sa'di says:

$$گر وزیر از خدا ترسیدے^{1}$$

Those in employment work very actively and diligently even for minor jobs, but as the time for prayer approaches, they recoil at the sight of water that is even somewhat cold. Why is this so? It is because hearts are devoid of the greatness of Allah Almighty. If people possessed even scant regard for the greatness of God Almighty and were cognizant and certain of death, all

---

[1] If only the vizier possessed fear of God. [Publisher]

their indolence and negligence would flee from them. Therefore, they should cultivate the **greatness** of God Almighty within their hearts and forever fear Him. He seizes fiercely. He overlooks and pardons, but when He takes hold of a person, He is firm to the extent that, لَا يَخَافُ عُقْبَهَا [1], that is to say, He does not care even for those who are left behind by such a one. On the contrary, Allah Almighty honours those and becomes a shield for those who fear Him and cultivate within their hearts His greatness.

It is recorded in the Hadith مَنْ كَانَ لِلّٰهِ كَانَ اللّٰهُ لَهُ, which means, Allah Almighty becomes one with those who become His. It is a pity, however, that many of those who pay heed and wish to gain the nearness of God Almighty **seek immediate results**. They know not the degree of patience and ambition that is required in matters of religion. It is surprising that they wait years on end for the acquisition of worldly objectives, for which they strive day in and day out, and for which they exert their best efforts. A farmer plants a seed and waits for quite some time, yet when it comes to matters of faith, they would like to be **transformed into saints** in

---

[1] *as-Shams,* 91:16 [Publisher]

a heartbeat. On the very first day, they expect to reach the throne of Allah, without undergoing any toil and hardship on this path, and without being subjected to trial.

Remember well, this is not the law and practice of God Almighty. Even in religious matters, every form of progress is gradual, and God Almighty cannot be pleased with mere declarations that we are Muslims or believers. As such He says:

اَحَسِبَ النَّاسُ اَنْ يُّتْرَكُوْٓا اَنْ يَّقُوْلُوْٓا اٰمَنَّا وَهُمْ لَا يُفْتَنُوْنَ [1]

That is, do these people think that Allah the Exalted will be pleased only because they claim to be believers and that they will be left alone, without being put to trial?

It is contrary to the practice of Allah to turn someone into a saint in an instant. If this had been God's way, the Holy Prophet, peace and blessings of Allah be upon him, would have done the same, and would have instantly turned his devoted companions into saints. He would not have allowed them to be put to trial and thus to have

---

[1] *al-Ankabut*, 29:3 [Publisher]

laid down their lives. Moreover, God Almighty would not have said the following about them:

مِنْهُمْ مَّنْ قَضٰى نَحْبَهٗ وَ مِنْهُمْ مَّنْ يَّنْتَظِرُ وَ مَا بَدَّلُوْا تَبْدِيْلًا ۙ [1]

Hence, when even worldly gains cannot be secured without hardship and toil, how utterly foolish then is one who considers faith to be easy. It is true that religion is a thing of ease, yet every blessing demands travail. Regardless, Islam is not overly demanding. Observe the Hindus, whose yogis and ascetics go to great lengths—their backs are broken while others grow out their nails. Likewise, **celibacy** was practiced by the Christians. Islam does not teach such practices but rather states:

قَدْ اَفْلَحَ مَنْ زَكّٰىهَا ۙ [2]

Meaning, a person who **purifies their soul** has attained salvation. In other words, one who abstains for the sake of God Almighty, from every kind of self-invented belief, sin, impiety, and from their base desires; who abandons every form of selfish pleasure, preferring hardships in the way of God; who gives precedence to

---

[1] There are *some* of them who have fulfilled their vow, and *some* who *still* wait, and they have not changed *their condition* in the least. (*al-Ahzab*, 33:24) [Publisher]

[2] *as-Shams*, 91:10 [Publisher]

God Almighty, discarding the world along with its luxuries,[1] is truly one who has attained salvation. Then Allah says:

$$\text{قَدْ خَابَ مَنْ دَسّٰهَا}^{2}$$

One who adulterates their soul and inclines to the earth, is reduced to dust. This single phrase is a summary of all the teachings of the Holy Quran and it expounds the manner in which a person can reach God Almighty.

It is a clear and established fact that until man renounces the misuse of his human faculties, he cannot find God. If you desire to escape the filth of this world and attain communion with God Almighty, then renounce these pleasures. For if not:

---

[1] **Footnote:** Badr reports: 'One who gives precedence to religion becomes one with God. A person ought to humble their soul, and God Almighty ought to be given precedence over everything. This is the essence of faith. One ought to renounce all forms of evil and only then does a person find God. (*Badr,* Volume 2, No. 6, dated 9 February 1906, p. 3)

[2] *as-Shams,* 91:11 [Publisher]

هم خدا خواہی وہم دنیائے دوں   ایں خیال است ومحال است و جنوں[1]

In actuality, human nature is not inherently evil nor is a thing evil in itself; rather, improper use makes it so. Display, for instance, is not bad in itself. For if one performs an action for the sake of God Almighty alone and so that others are moved to perform that good deed as well, then such an exhibition is also virtuous.

There are two forms of display. Firstly, for the sake of the world. For instance, when a person is leading the congregational prayer, and a high-ranking person joins the congregation, he begins to prolong the prayer in view and consideration of the latter's presence. On such an instance, some from among the congregation become overwhelmed with awe, and in turn, the person leading the prayer swells with pride. This is also a kind of ostentation, which is not always manifested, except on particular occasions like one who eats bread at a time of hunger, or one who drinks water at a time of thirst. On the contrary, however, one who beautifies their prayer

---

[1] *You seek God as well as this wretched world; this is wishful thinking, rather impossible, nay insanity.* [Publisher]

only for the sake of God Almighty is free from ostentation. In fact, this is a means of seeking divine pleasure. So display too has its occasions and man is a creature that instinctively abstains from improper action. For instance, a person who considers himself to be truly virtuous and pious is travelling alone and comes across a pouch of jewels. He looks at it and realises that there is no one around and no one can see him. If on such occasion the person does not fall upon the money, considering it to be the right of another and belonging to someone else, and thus refrains from taking it, not being driven by greed, then such a one has acted with true virtue and piety. Otherwise, if nothing but mere claims exist, his true character will be revealed on such an occasion and he will take the money. Similarly, a person about whom it is believed that they are free from pretentions, will only be proven as such when they do not exhibit ostentation even when an opportunity arises.

However, as I have just described, sometimes these habits are performed on such occasions that they become virtues. As such, there is somewhat of an element of **display** in a person who offers the congregational prayer. However, this would only be ostentatious when one's purpose is to show others. If, on the other hand, the purpose is obedience to Allah and His Messenger, then this becomes a marvellous blessing. So observe your prayers both at mosques and in your homes. Similarly, if on a particular occasion, contributions are being sought for a religious endeavour and one observes that others do not rise to the occasion and remain unmoved, and such a person leads in making a contribution only so that others may be motivated to do the same, this would apparently be an act of display, yet still warrants spiritual reward.

Likewise, God Almighty states in the Holy Quran:

$$ \text{لَا تَمْشِ فِى الْأَرْضِ مَرَحًا} \ ^1 $$

This means, walk not in the earth haughtily. However, it is recorded in the Hadith that during battle, a person was strutting forward with a puffed chest. Upon observing this, the Holy Prophet, peace and blessings of Allah be upon him, said that this act is displeasing to God Almighty, but on an occasion like this, it pleases Him. Thus:

---

[1] *Luqman*, 31:19 [Publisher]

44

گر حفظِ مراتب نہ کنی زندیقی[1]

Thus, an action performed on its appropriate occasion makes one a believer, but if performed inappropriately, makes one a disbeliever. As I have stated previously, no trait is evil in itself; rather, inappropriate use makes it so.

It is reported with relation to Hazrat Umar, Allah be pleased with him, that someone asked him about his anger and remarked that he was a man of fiery disposition prior to his acceptance of Islam. Hazrat Umar responded by saying that the anger is just as before, albeit, in the past it would manifest itself inappropriately, but now it is exercised at the appropriate occasion. Islam enjoins the use of every faculty at its proper place. Therefore, one should never allow one's faculties to wither away, instead, learn their proper use. Those who abide by the teaching of turning the cheek after being slapped on the other, adhere to flawed and idealistic tenets. It is possible that this teaching was earlier a law **specific to time and place**. However, this law can neither be for all times, nor can it be applied successfully. For a human being is like a tree with branches that

---

[1] If you do not observe appropriate etiquette, you are a disbeliever. [Publisher]

spread in all directions. If only one branch were tended
to, the others would be ruined and destroyed. The flaw
in this teaching of Christianity is clearly evident. How
can it nurture all the faculties of man? If forgiveness had
been the only trait of merit, why then was man endowed
with the **faculty of retribution,** along with others?
Moreover, why then is this teaching of forgiveness not
being practiced? Islam, on the other hand, has presented
the perfect teaching, which we have received through
the Holy Prophet, peace and blessings of Allah be upon
him, and that is:

جَزَّؤُاسَيِّئَةٍ سَيِّئَةٌ مِّثْلُهَا فَمَنْ عَفَا وَ اَصْلَحَ فَاَجْرُهُ عَلَى اللهِ [1]

That is, the recompense of an injury is an injury the like
thereof, but whoso forgives sin...[2] when it is likely to
bring about reformation and does not lead to any form
of disorder, their reward is with Allah Almighty.

This clearly demonstrates that the Holy Quran does not
at all advocate useless forbearance and resistance from
exacting retribution in all circumstances. Instead, divine
will teaches one to judge the situation and determine

---

[1] *ash-Shura,* 42:41 [Publisher]
[2] Word(s) omitted due to scribal error. [Publisher]

whether an occasion calls for wrongdoing to be pardoned and forgiven, or punished. If punishment is prudent on the occasion, it ought to be administered in proportion to the wrongdoing. However, if the occasion calls for forgiveness, the thought of punishment ought to be abandoned.

The excellence of this teaching is that it takes into consideration all circumstances. If, in compliance with the Gospel, every evil and wicked person were set free, anarchy would erupt in the world. Therefore, always bear in mind that none of your faculties are to be viewed as dead; rather, strive to exercise them on the appropriate occasion. I truly say that this teaching is a reflection of human faculties. Pity those who are enamoured by the sweet words of the Christians and have given up a bounty the like of Islam. A truthful person does not appear sweet to others on all occasions, just as a mother cannot constantly spoil her child with sweets. Rather, when the need arises, she administers bitter medicine as well. Such is the state of a truthful reformer. It is this very teaching that is blessed in every aspect. Our God is one who is truthful. Even the Christians believe in our God. All others are compelled to believe in those attributes of God that we accept. At one place, in his book, Reverend Pfander raises the question about how such people would be called to account on the Day of Judgement who dwell in an island where the message of Christianity had not yet reached. He then provides a response himself and states that they would not be asked whether or not they believed in Christ and in his atonement; rather, they would be asked whether they believed in the God of Islam, who is described as being One and without partner.

Even those who dwell in the forest are instinctively compelled to believe in the God of Islam. Everyone's conscience and inner light testifies that they ought to believe in the God of Islam. The Muslims of today have forgotten the essence and true teachings of Islam as expounded earlier, but I have been tasked with its re-establishment. This alone is the magnificent purpose of my advent.

Apart from the issues mentioned earlier, there are other academic and theological errors, which continue to spread among the Muslims, and our task is to remove them. For instance, they believe that only Jesus and his mother are free from the touch of Satan while all others, God-forbid, are not. This is a blatant error, nay, it amounts to disbelief and is an extreme dishonour to the Holy Prophet, peace and blessings of Allah be upon him. Those who concoct such ideologies are bereft of even the slightest indignation. They seek to disgrace Islam. Indeed, such people are far from Islam. In actual fact, it is evident from the Holy Quran that there are two kinds of birth. One is with the touch of the Holy Spirit and the other with the touch of Satan. The children of all those who are pious and righteous are born with the touch of the Holy Spirit. Children that come from sin are born with the touch of Satan. All the Prophets were born with the touch of the Holy Spirit. However, the Jews alleged that God-forbid, Jesus was an illegitimate child who was born out of Mary's illicit relation with a soldier named Panthera,[1] and so he was a result of the touch of Satan. For this reason, in order to absolve Jesus from this allegation, Allah Almighty testified in his favour and said that he too was born with the touch of the Holy Spirit. Since no such allegation was raised against our Noble Prophet, peace and blessings of Allah

---

[1] The Roman soldier Tiberius Iulius Abdes Panthera (c. 22 BC – AD 40). The name, 'Pantera,' which is a variant form of this name also appears in certain texts. [Publisher]

be upon him, nor any other Prophet, there was no need to make the above statement about them.

Abdullah and Aminah, the parents of our Noble Prophet, peace and blessings of Allah be upon him, had always been held in high esteem, and no one had ever entertained any sort of mistrust and suspicion about them. Testimony is required only to exonerate a person who falls into the clutches of a lawsuit, but as for one who is free from the grip of litigation, no such testimony is required.

Similarly, there is another error that has crept into the Muslims and it relates to the *Mi'raj.*[1] We believe that the Holy Prophet, peace and blessings of Allah be upon him, experienced the *Mi'raj,* but it is wrong to believe, as some people do, that this was nothing more than an ordinary dream. Likewise, it is false to believe that the Holy Prophet went to heaven with his physical body. The true and correct belief is that the *Mi'raj* was a kind of vision, experienced with a body made of light. There was a body, but it was spiritual; there was a state of wakefulness, but spiritual, in the form of a vision. This

---

[1] A spiritual experience of the Holy Prophet, peace and blessings of Allah be upon him, in which he travelled to the heavens. [Publisher]

cannot be comprehended by the people of this world, except for those who have undergone such an experience.

The Jews also demanded the miracle of ascending bodily to heaven in a state of wakefulness from the Holy Prophet[sa]. The Holy Quran responds to this as follows:

قُلْ سُبْحَانَ رَبِّيْ هَلْ كُنْتُ اِلَّا بَشَرًا رَّسُوْلًا ¹

Say [O Muhammad[sa]], Holy is my Lord. I am not but a man sent as a Messenger; mortals never fly to heaven. This is the practice of Allah, which has existed since time immemorial.

Another error which exists among a vast majority of Muslims is that they give precedence to the Hadith over the Holy Quran while it is wrong to do so. The Holy Quran possesses a rank of certainty while the Hadith possess an element of conjecture. The Hadith are not a judge over the Holy Quran, rather, it is the Holy Quran that stands as an authority over the Hadith. Nevertheless, the Hadith are an exposition of the Holy Quran and ought to be given their due rank. It is incumbent to

---

¹ *Bani Isra'il,* 17:94 [Publisher]

believe in a Hadith so long as it accords with and does not oppose the Holy Quran. However, if a Hadith contradicts the Holy Quran, then such a statement is no Hadith at all but is rather a worthless statement. Nevertheless, the Hadith are crucial in order to understand the Holy Quran. For the divine commandments revealed in the Holy Quran were first put into practice by the Holy Prophet, peace and blessings of Allah be upon him, and then practiced by others under his instruction. In this manner the Holy Prophet set an example. If this example had not existed, Islam could not have been understood. Still, the primary source remains the Holy Quran. Some who experience visions hear directly from the Holy Prophet, peace and blessings of Allah be upon him, such Hadith that others have not yet come to know of, or are able to confirm the authenticity of Hadith already present.

Hence, many such things are found to exist among these people, which are diametrically opposed to Islamic practice and due to which God Almighty is displeased. And so, Allah Almighty no longer considers them to be Muslim, unless they denounce these false doctrines and return to the right path. It is for this purpose that God Almighty has commissioned me so that I may remove all of these errors and so that I may re-establish true Islam in the world.

This is the difference between these people and us. Their condition no longer accords with the essence of Islam. They have become like a ruined and barren garden. Their hearts are impure. God Almighty desires to create a new people who will become a model of the true Islam by embracing the truth and righteousness.

The end [1]

(Al-Hakam, 17th February, 17th May, 17th June 1906

---

[1] *Al-Hakam*, Volume 10, No. 21, dated 17 June 1906, pp. 3-4